Scrapman
and the Incredible Flying Machine

Carolyn Bear

Illustrated by John Prater

Chapter 1

Scrapman was a mechanical man.
He lived with Winston who
owned a scrap-yard. Scrapman
was made out of odds and ends
that Winston had saved from
old broken machines.

His brain was made from a
personal organiser that someone
had thrown away because it
was always going wrong.

It still went wrong, but now
Scrapman went wrong with it.

'Od ear,' said Scrapman.

Winston was working late. So late,
that he was having his supper heated
over a gas ring in the shed.

Scrapman was opening a tin of
baked beans for him. At least he
thought it was a tin of baked beans.

'Volly od beans,' said Scrapman.

'I can't eat that,' said Winston, in a tired kind of voice. 'Can't you read what it says on the label?'

Scrapman hung his head. He wasn't very good at reading. He could read his name and a few really easy words but he couldn't read what it said on the cat food tin.

Scrapcat was watching from under the workbench.

He didn't eat cat food either because he was a mechanical cat and he worked on batteries, not cat food.

Scrapman went and sat in the corner. He felt very sad. He wished he could read like Emma. Emma was his special friend. She was teaching him to talk like a human being. She had a picture book with wonderful stories in it about robots. These were mechanical men like him but they could do amazing things.

They could drive rockets and walk on the moon and save people from fires and floods and earthquakes. Scrapman loved looking at the pictures, but he had to wait until Emma came round to find out what the stories were about.

Scrapcat saw that Scrapman was sad, so he went and sat beside him.

Winston opened a proper tin of beans and he put the tin of cat food in the rubbish bin. While he wasn't looking, Scrapman took it out.

He'd bought it as a treat for Patch. Patch was Emma's cat. He liked to come and play with Scrapcat while Emma was at school. He'd climb in through the window when Winston and Scrapman were busy.

Then he'd show Scrapcat how to do
useful cat things, like chasing pieces of
string and hiding things under the
workbench.

Now, you may be wondering why
Winston and Scrapman were so busy.
They were working round the clock on
Winston's incredible invention.

It was a wonderful flying machine
that didn't need petrol to make it fly.
It was worked by pedals like a bicycle.
It was almost finished. Just a few more
nuts and bolts to fix and it would be
ready for a test flight.

But where had those last few nuts
and bolts gone?

Chapter 2

At last, the day came for the first test flight. Winston had cleared a runway through the scrap-yard.

The runway led out into a field, and beyond that there was another field, so there was plenty of room to take off.

That morning, Winston took off one of his socks and hung it on a pole to test the wind direction.

It was an east wind, steady and strong, just right for testing a plane.

Emma arrived early with Patch.
She'd brought a special picnic and
a big bottle of fizzy lemonade
to celebrate after the flight. She
found Winston and Scrapman busy
underneath the machine, making
some last-minute checks. Scrapcat was
running in and out through
his scrapflap giving
up-to-the-minute
reports on the
weather.

By ten o'clock in the morning,
Winston said that everything was
ready.

It was going to be cold up there in
the sky, so he put on a thick jacket
with a woolly lining over his overalls.
And he wore his special goggles to
protect his eyes from the wind.

'Open the doors,' he said proudly to
Scrapman. 'Stand well back,' he said to
Emma and Patch.

And then, very carefully, Winston and Scrapman pushed the flying machine out into the open.

A small crowd had gathered outside. People had heard about the flying machine. They had come to share in the excitement of seeing it take off for the first time.

Winston held up a hand for silence. 'Welcome,' he said. Then he said something about this being a 'historic occasion' and everyone clapped and some people cheered. One little boy waved the sock on the pole like a flag.

Winston climbed up into the flying machine and Scrapman started to climb up behind him.

'Stop!' said Winston. 'You can't come with me, Scrapman. You're too big. The machine could never get off the ground with you in it.'

'Od ear,' said Scrapman. He climbed down feeling very big and clumsy.

Emma went and held his hand to make him feel better and Scrapcat rubbed himself up against his legs.

Winston tested the flaps and jiggled the joystick and looked in his mirrors to check that everything was working properly. Then he pulled down his goggles and turned up his collar. He waved proudly to the crowd.

'Chocks away!' he called out, and Emma and Scrapman pulled out the bricks from under the wheels.

Winston started to pedal. The flying machine began to move forward.

He pedalled faster and the machine
picked up speed. Everyone in the
crowd held their breath as the flying
machine shot down the runway.
It got faster and faster. Winston
was pedalling like mad
and going red in
the face.

The machine reached the first field. It was going very fast indeed, but it didn't take off. It reached the second field going faster still and it got to the very end of that...

But it still didn't take off.

'Od ear,' Scrapman.

One hour later, Winston was ready to try again.

'I need your help, Scrapman,' he said. He took off his warm woolly lined jacket and handed it to Scrapman. Scrapman looked hopeful. Maybe this time he would have a chance to go up in the incredible flying machine.

But no such luck. Winston took off his boots, and his other sock and even his watch. He wanted to make the flying machine lighter.

'Scrapman, this time I want you to get behind and push,' he said. 'The machine has to go much faster before it can get off the ground.'

Scrapman handed Winston's warm woolly jacket, the boots, the sock and the watch to Emma and got his shoulder behind the machine.

'Chocks away!' shouted Winston
again.

The machine got under way much
faster this time. Scrapman was pushing
as hard as he could. His legs were
going so fast you could hardly see
them. The crowd got excited and
started clapping.

The little boy waved the sock on the pole. The people cheered as the machine sped across the first field. And the next field. It was going so fast, it left Scrapman behind.

But it still didn't take off.

By the time they had pedalled the machine back to the scrap-yard the crowd had given up and gone home. Scrapman and Winston pushed it back into the shed.

One of the wheels had come loose. Winston said the machine probably needed a good oiling before it could fly.

Winston seemed depressed.

Emma laid out the picnic on a cloth, but although they were very good sandwiches and nice fizzy lemonade, it wasn't the celebration they'd been looking forward to.

Then Scrapman remembered the tin of food he'd saved as a treat for Patch. And although everyone else was depressed, Patch was happy.

Winston spent the afternoon in the shed mending the wheel of the incredible flying machine and oiling every joint. He had a worried look on his face and he said he didn't want any help. He didn't whistle while he was working, which was a *bad sign*.

Scrapman and Emma sat on the grass feeling bored. After a while, Scrapman asked Emma if she would read him a story from her big picture book.

'Scrapman, you should try to learn to read. Then you could read the book for yourself,' said Emma.

Scrapman didn't feel like learning to read. He wanted to help Winston.

More than anything, he wanted
to fly up in the sky in the incredible
flying machine. He felt cross. What
was the point in reading about robots
doing all these incredible things, when
he wasn't allowed to do anything?

'Look, Scrapman,' said Emma,
pointing to a word on the page.
'R.o.b.o.t. What does that spell?'

'I dun no,' said Scrapman crossly.

'Robot,' said Emma. 'You see. It's easy.'

But it wasn't easy for Scrapman.

'C.a.t.,' said Emma, trying something easier. Scrapcat sat up and pricked up his ears and nudged Scrapman.

'Cat?' asked Scrapman.

'Very good,' said Emma. 'Now how about d.o.g.?'

'I dun no,' said Scrapman. 'You read the story, M.R.'

'Scrapman, you're not even trying,' said Emma. 'I'm not going to read to you if you won't try.'

And she got up and cleared up the picnic. Then she picked up Patch and went home.

Chapter 3

That night, Winston finished work on the flying machine.

He wiped his hands on an oily rag and said with a sigh: 'Scrapman, my old lad, it may never take off from the ground. But it's a fine machine all the same.' And he went off home for a good night's sleep.

Scrapman didn't sleep. He sat turning the pages of the picture book and looking at the pictures.

How he would love to have
adventures and do brave things like
the robots in the stories. He traced a
finger along the words that Emma had
been reading to him.

'R.o.b.o.t,' he spelt out. 'Robot!'

Maybe it wasn't so difficult after all.

He sat trying to puzzle out the words
of his favourite story. Emma had read
it to him over and over again so he
almost knew it by heart.

He couldn't read all of the words but
he could read enough to remember the
story.

He fell asleep with his head on the
open page of the book.

The next morning,
Scrapman woke up and
wondered where he was.
Then he looked at the book
and remembered that he
could read. He felt so proud
of himself. Nothing was too
difficult for him now. He felt
as if he could do *anything*.
He stood up and stretched
and looked around
the shed.

The incredible flying machine was standing in the early morning light. The sun was shining on its fresh new paint.

That's when Scrapman had an idea. He would give Winston the biggest surprise of his life. He wasn't too big and heavy and clumsy to fly. He could do incredible things like the robots in the book. He would prove it. He would show the world.

So Scrapman woke up Scrapcat and the two of them set to work.

Very quietly, they opened the doors of the shed and pushed the incredible flying machine out into the yard.

It was a fine morning. The birds were singing on the telegraph wires. Winston's sock was stretched out in the breeze, showing that the wind was set in just the right direction.

'O volly good,' said Scrapman and he went back into the shed. He put on Winston's warm woolly jacket and went back to the flying machine.

Scrapcat had already jumped up into the back seat and was waiting expectantly.

'Get down, Scrapcat,' said Scrapman. 'Cats don't fly.' And he made Scrapcat jump down and wait on the ground.

Scrapman tried to remember
everything that Winston had done.
He jiggled the flaps and wobbled the
joystick. He checked in his mirrors.
Then he leaned out and gave Scrapcat
a rather grand wave.

'Chocks away!' he shouted and
Scrapcat pushed the bricks away from
under the wheels.

Scrapman started pedalling.

The flying machine shot off down the runway.

Scrapcat belted after it and with one giant leap he jumped in behind Scrapman.

Scrapman didn't notice. He was pedalling as hard as he could. The machine went faster and faster. Scrapman's legs were going round like pistons, which wasn't surprising because they *were* pistons.

They were going so fast that you couldn't even see them. They were just a blur. And then, as they got to the first field, the flying machine started to lift very gently off the ground.

Scrapman was so surprised that he stopped pedalling and the machine bumped down on the ground again. So Scrapman pedalled hard once more and sure enough, the machine started to lift off into the air.

It lifted *just* high enough to clear the hedge at the end of the second field.

Incredible as it seemed – *they were in the air!*

But it wasn't so incredible really because although Scrapman didn't have a very good brain, he was very very strong. He was ten times as strong as an ordinary man, which meant, unlike Winston, Scrapman could pedal fast enough to get the flying machine off the ground.

The cows in the meadow stopped munching grass when they saw the strange flying machine zooming over them and started moo-ing. The sheep ran in a little frightened woolly bunch to the far end of their field, baaa-ing to each other. The crows left the telegraph wires and flew in a noisy flock around the machine.

'Hip-hop-haroo,'
shouted Scrapman.

And Scrapcat poked his head out of
the back seat and went: 'Honk, honk.'

Which made Scrapman jump so
hard he swerved the plane so that it
turned in a great circle and flew back
across the scrap-yard.

Chapter 4

Winston woke up to a strange noise. It sounded as if a zoo had been let loose in the fields behind the scrap-yard. He went out in his pyjamas to see what the matter was.

That's when the incredible flying machine zoomed overhead.

Winston rubbed his eyes, he scratched his head, his mouth fell open. He couldn't believe what he was seeing.

There was the incredible flying machine. And it was up in the air. And – no – *yes* – that was *Scrapman* flying it.

'Come down, Scrapman!' shouted Winston and he waved his arms. But Scrapman couldn't hear him. He just pedalled harder and the flying machine went faster.

Emma was cleaning her teeth in the bathroom when the incredible flying machine went past her window. She couldn't believe her eyes. Surely that couldn't be Scrapman flying it? She dropped her toothbrush and ran out into the garden.

'Come down, Scrapman!' she shouted. And Patch, who had seen Scrapcat in the back seat, wound himself around her legs and miaowed loudly – cats don't fly.

Scrapman felt very proud when he saw Emma waving at him and pedalled faster still. And the flying machine rose higher.

So Emma ran down the lane to Winston's scrap-yard and Patch ran along behind her.

When she got there, she found a worried crowd of people gathered round Winston.

'What are we going to do?' asked Emma.

'I don't know,' said Winston.

That's when the police arrived. The chief policeman took his notebook out of his pocket and said, 'You'll have to get him down. We can't have flying machines buzzing around the sky. It's not safe.'

'But how?' said Winston. 'He's too high up to hear me.'

That's when someone thought of calling the fire-engine.

When the firemen came they stretched their ladder to its full length and Winston climbed up to the top.

Next time Scrapman came round,
Winston waved his arms and shouted,
'Come down, Scrapman!'

Scrapman heard him this time.

'Od ear,' he said.

You see, he knew how to get the
flying machine up. *But he didn't know
how to get it down.*

Chapter 5

Scrapman started to panic, so he pedalled even faster. Now he was going so fast he was afraid he would hit something. He made wider and wider circles round the church and then he headed out into the open country.

'We must follow him,' said the chief policeman and he got back into his car.

Winston and Emma and Patch jumped into Winston's van and followed the police car.

The firemen got into the fire-engine
and followed the van, and most of the
people who had gathered to see what
was going on, followed *them*.

The police car went first with its blue
light flashing and its siren blaring and
the procession of cars followed. Off
they went through the winding
country lanes.

They had to go very fast indeed to keep up with the flying machine.

'Od ear, od ear,' said Scrapman when he saw the police car and the fire-engine and all the cars chasing after him. He pedalled even faster.

The flying machine led the procession miles out into the country and then it led them all the way back again.

Emma looked out of the van window.

'Poor Scrapman,' she said. 'He looks scared. I don't think he knows how to come down.'

'But it's simple,' said Winston. 'He only has to slow down and the machine will come down. All he needs is a big open field to land in.'

They were just driving up to Emma's school playing field. This was a big open field. There was a mowing machine in it and it had just started noisily to mow the grass.

'Stop!' shouted Emma. She'd had an idea.

Winston screeched to a halt and Emma ran over to the man on the big noisy mowing machine.

Winston didn't know what was going on. He could see Scrapman up in the sky. The flying machine was coming closer and closer.

He could see Emma waving her arms.

Scrapman didn't come down
immediately.

He had to circle the field three times
before the flying machine was low
enough and slow enough to land.

Everyone held their breath as it
came to earth with a bump and a jolt –
and then skidded to a halt.

Emma ran across and put her arms
around Scrapman, which was difficult
because she only came up to his knees.
Scrapcat jumped out and Patch came
over and licked his face in a friendly
kind of way.

Winston stood with his hands on his
hips.

Scrapman hung his head and waited
to hear what Winston was going to
say.

Scrapman thought Winston was going to be very angry indeed.

'Well, well, well,' said Winston. 'I didn't think the flying machine would ever get off the ground.'

'I dun no how it ever got down,' said Scrapman.

Then Winston slapped him on the back. 'Well done, my old lad. So who taught you to read?' he asked.

'M.R.,' said Scrapman.

'In that case,' said Winston, 'I think Emma should be the very first person to go up with you in the flying machine. Just once, mind. Very carefully, round the church and back again.'

So Scrapman and Scrapcat and Patch and Emma climbed into the flying machine and Scrapman flew them in a perfect circle round the village.

About the author

I receive a lot of letters
from schools asking me
for further adventures of
Scrapman. And I'm often
sent wonderful ideas
from children suggesting
brave and clever things that Scrapman
might do.

But Scrapman's adventures don't
always turn out the way he'd like
them to. Od ear!